Securing Our Union

CHOOSING THE RIGHT PARTNER FOR A STABLE, HEALTHY, AND HAPPY MARRIAGE

TAMEIKA ALLEN DAVIS

© 2017 Divine Works Publishing
ALL RIGHTS RESERVED

All rights reserved. No part of this publication may be reproduced, stored in a retrieval system, or transmitted in any form or by any means, electronic, mechanical, photocopying, recording or otherwise without the prior permission of the publisher or in accordance with the provisions of the Copyright, Designs, and Patents Act 1988 or under the terms of any license permitting limited copying issued by the Copyright Licensing Agency.

ISBN-13: 978-0-9996047-4-8

Published by:
Divine Works Publishing
Royal Palm Beach, Florida USA
www.divineworkspublishing.com
561-990-BOOK (2665)

Dedication

This book is dedicated to all the single females who are waiting for their ideal partner to show up. Don't lose faith!

You, my friend, are being prepared...

Acknowledgments

I first would like to acknowledge my husband, Marcel E.K. Davis *a.k.a* Jason, for being a true supporter of my dream in writing my first book and for providing the subject matter. It is because of our union that I can now spread hope and help shed the light of true love to others.

I also want to acknowledge Divine Works Publishing for being an inspiration when they hosted the ICABA Authors Reception event in South Florida. It was there that I derived the inspiration to start writing this book.

Additionally, I would like to acknowledge the family members who have been supportive of my goals and dreams since childhood. One can never place a value on a having a safe, healthy, and solid foundation to grow upon.

A GREAT BIG THANKS TO YOU ALL!

Introduction

I was moved to write this book after attending an event in my home town which showcased the success of various authors and their most recent works. During this one event, we listened to the different authors each share how they began their writing journeys. One author was inspired to write after overcoming several career and personal difficulties which instilled in her the ability to find peace amidst life's adversities. Another, attributed her inspiration to other writers whom she enjoyed reading and was thankful for the impact their writing had upon her life. Yet another, began writing because he witnessed his hard-working mother's struggle to behold the American dream unfold before his very eyes. Now, I am so fired up about this book because I get to share with you a little about myself and our marriage journey.

I have always desired to write, but never had any real inspiration to start. I journaled while in High School and during College, but kept it hidden for my own viewing. I would jot down things that had a major impact on my life. I would basically journal to help me release stress or anxiety. I recall writing about my first trip, my first day in college, a secret crush I had, my family relational dynamics, and finally my marriage. I am pleased to be at this place where I am confident to share our story and to inspire others in the same way I was inspired.

By sharing our experiences, we hope to shed some light and bring clarity to those seeking to be married or who may already be married and are experiencing a degree of difficulty especially pertaining to the involvement and perhaps forced opinions of others.

Contents

CHAPTER ONE 1
MY PRIME AGE: KNOW WHO YOU ARE

CHAPTER TWO 7
HIS PRIME AGE: KNOW WHO HE IS

CHAPTER THREE 11
SOCIALIZATION & INTEGRATION: IDENTIFYING YOUR MATE THROUGH SOCIAL INTERACTION

CHAPTER FOUR 17
DATING EXPERIENCES: KNOW YOUR LIKES AND DISLIKES

CHAPTER FIVE 23
FAMILY RELATIONS & MARRIAGE BELIEFS: DO YOU SHARE THE SAME BELIEFS?

CHAPTER SIX 29
OUR UNION: CHOOSING YOUR MATE WITHOUT EXTERNAL INFLUENCES

CHAPTER SEVEN 37
SECURING OUR UNION: STAYING COMMITTED AND TRUE TO EACH OTHER

CHAPTER EIGHT 43
SUMMARY: MAINTAINING A HEALTHY RELATIONSHIP

Chapter One

MY PRIME AGE: KNOW WHO YOU ARE

I was born on a beautiful island; if you can imagine the most beautiful island in the Caribbean then you've got it. The island of Jamaica is well known for its scenic landscape, delicious blue mountain coffee, and its upbeat rhythmic music. Being raised there instilled in me certain core values that dictated what I expected from myself and from others. These values would later determine who I believed would make the most suitable partner for me. For me, these core values and beliefs were love, forgiveness, hard work, achievement, prayer and domestication. My ideal partner would have to value these things as well.

My foundational understanding of love was shaped through the many hours of which I sat through church services and classes receiving biblical teachings and instructions. That understanding was further reinforced through the love I received from my family and friends. **Love, when it is pure, is felt and does not need to be explained.** All of these experiences helped to set an expectation for my future.

Coupled with my understanding of love, came the necessity to forgive and forgive quickly. Through personal experiences and the shared experiences of others, I learned about the healing power of forgiveness (*especially when exercised after major disagreements*). Forgiveness is something that is vital to my makeup and something that a life partner would have to equally value. For me, the ability to forgive is a trait of a mature individual and of someone who is ready to tackle the challenges that relationships can bring.

Hard work was yet another character trait that was ingrained in me as a child. One that I mastered through my compelling desire to excel and become a positive role model for others. I enjoyed being honored for high achievements and pushing myself further. Thus, whoever was a close friend or potential mate would have to encourage this in me as I would also encourage the same in them.

I also learned the power of prayer by observing my grandmother pray morning, noon, and night. Not a day went by that she would miss her prayer time. I admired her commitment and adoration to a higher power. I remember having to be brave at a young age because I lived in a rural area far from my inner-city school. By the age of seven, I traveled to school alone because this was customary on the island. Praying for guidance became second nature to me when facing any trials along the way. I am so thankful for the example that she set.

On school days, I was awakened as early as 5:30am in the morning; my mother would help me dress and then escorted me to the front door. I'd have to make my own way to the bus stop which was a bit of a journey from home. I learned to be brave and courageous from a young age. I was encouraged by my teachers to excel and I took their advise seriously–although at times, I'd be teased for being the "teachers pet"–but I really didn't mind. I felt criticized, at times, because of my ability and persistence, and learned from an early age that I would have to guard my ambitions as it would make others feel insecure. In my culture there is a saying that goes "yuh gwaan like yuh too nice", which simply means that one is carrying themselves in a prideful and dignified way, which is not accepted as the norm amongst those who are not striving for more. As a young child, I could never understand why that was a problem. Yet, despite the challenges I faced, I was always a high achiever and remained firm in realizing my goals. My faith in a higher power has helped me to believe in myself and has inspired me to always give my best. So naturally, I would need a partner who would understand that and believe the same.

Later, a sense of healthy competition would be cultivated within me. I have a cousin, her name is Ashley, who had become competitive towards me and her Mother Gina made it her duty to have her participate in every event or competition that I was involved in. It was interesting because my mother pushed me to do my best in everything that I did. Although competition can create strife, it can also be used in a constructive way to help push yourself further. I remember feeling it was frustrating at that time, but as I grew older I learned to appreciate it. Being competitive has helped me to aim higher and aiming higher has helped me to achieve more. I would say that healthy competition has helped me to become more successful.

Overall, my childhood was gratifying and I was fortunate enough to enjoy those years. I played popular childhood games with my cousins and friends in our family home. I would spend countless hours playing outside enjoying nature, sometimes riding a bike along the countryside and picking from a variety of seasonal fruits. Most of my family members are great cooks so a nice island cuisine was always a delectable experience at dinner time. Although I enjoyed my childhood, at a young age I also learned the importance of responsibility and domestication and by the age of 9 I already knew how to cook by carefully observing my mother in the kitchen. Preparation for my future was well underway as I also completed loads of laundry and was responsible for numerous household chores. My family, at times, would express their pride as they watched me evolve into a well-trained, responsible young woman. Being responsible from such an early age helped me to become independent and independence became another very important attribute for me in seeking a life partner.

Later, an opportunity to attend one of the top ranking schools in the local area was afforded me. It was a very good school. The teachers and mentors who believed in me were great and helped to shape my future in ways that I could never fully thank them for. I passed the common entrance exam, which is almost equivalent to the SAT's, on my first attempt by the age of 11 years old which granted me access to William Knibb High School. This achievement signified a great moment of success for me and allowed me to skip the sixth grade. I remember again my parents being so proud. Hence, the concepts of love, hard work, a sense of achievement, and independence were themes repeated throughout my childhood.

Questions to Consider

- List 3 to 5 of your core values:

- Do you recall which childhood experiences (negative or positive) helped to reinforce these values in you?

- Which positive traits did you develop from being around your family?

- Which negative traits did you develop from being around your family?

- List the key people who helped shape your beliefs and character during childhood:

- Which of their traits do you see in yourself that you admire? Which would you like to improve?

Chapter Two

HIS PRIME AGE: KNOW WHO HE IS

My husband grew up in a small area of the island where he was raised by his mother, aunts, and grandparents. He was known to be very witty. He too, has always been bold and courageous—an explorer by nature. He also journeyed to school alone from his home district by the early age of seven. He would go to school and return home without permission and without injury. He would craft small gadgets to bring with him to school, and even though it got him into trouble plenty of times, it never stopped him. He was very creative. He enjoyed hanging with his friends, picking exotic fruits from his neighbor's trees, and going around sharing them with others. He spent a lot of time with his aunts and as a result he is thoroughly domesticated. He attended Georges, an all boys school, where he was recognized as one of the top students within his class. He participated in a number of extracurricular activities such as drama, singing, and arts.

He migrated to the United States at the age of 15, where he resided with his mother in Chicago, while he attended the college of DuPage to complete his undergraduate studies. He became a successful mortgage broker while still attending college and purchased his first house by the age of 24. He traveled regularly to North America, Mexico, Canada and the Bahamas. He moved to Florida with his father for about a year prior to purchasing his home so that he could experience another state prior to deciding to settle down. After the housing market crash of 2008, he became a Licensed Practical Nurse. Success in the mortgage industry had become defunct. Luckily, he enjoys nursing and is passionate about what he does and he always strives to deliver the best care possible. He later became a registered nurse and a business entrepreneur.

It's not hard to see we share many values and beliefs about life, and how he possesses so many of the attributes which I admire.

Questions to Consider

- In which geographical region was your partner raised and by whom?

- How has this helped shaped their core beliefs and value system?

- List 3 to 5 character traits that "you" believe are related to their core values.

- How have these traits impacted your relationship?

- Do you share enough of the same ideals and values to build a foundation that will serve you both?

Chapter Three

SOCIALIZATION & INTEGRATION: IDENTIFYING YOUR MATE THROUGH SOCIAL INTERACTION

One of the most impactful experiences of my life occurred when I moved to London, UK. It was an amazing time because I was 14 years old and up until this point in my life I had only experienced one culture—my own. A culture which comprises a population of 90% black, 1% East Indian, 9% mixed and is sprinkled with a few people of Caucasian and Chinese descent. The official language spoken is English, but the majority speak a broken dialect otherwise known as *patois*.

My country was once a Spanish colony (during the early centuries), but later became a British colony, and as fate would have it, I traveled to Great Britain at 14 years of age. I was forever changed by the entire experience. It was my first time on a plane. My young thoughts caused me to think that areas outside my small island were full of life and goodness. I had always heard the term "the grass is greener on the other side" and I literally believed it. I was living with my aunt Valery when my mother received the call from my father to visit "foreign". I didn't grow up with my father, so every interaction or communication with him brought sheer excitement. He had migrated to the United States when I was a toddler and he was calling to report that I would be moving to live with my grandmother in England to afford me better opportunities. I was ecstatic about traveling from a small island to a great big country. I didn't know what was going to happen, but I knew it would be better than what I was used to. Although I had a good childhood experience, I always felt that there was more. My mother was a single parent who worked very hard to send both me and my younger brother Aston to school. We grew up in a one bedroom located in an urban area and traveled a far distance to get to and from the city. Yet, I have no regrets because I always believe everything that happens in life gives us an opportunity to grow, develop, and expand.

It was an exciting time for me to travel, but I felt sad about leaving behind my family, my friends, and the life that I had grown familiar with. I cried on my way to the airport, but they were tears of joy and sadness mixed together. I remembered going to the summer fest at school and hanging with friends doing various outdoor activities. I would miss it all, but I had to let go and embrace the unknown which awaited me. My flight was scheduled for mid-day on a bright summer day and I remember my mother dropping me off at the airport and waving goodbye. I felt an influx of mixed emotions. I arrived early morning in London after a nine hour flight to the Heathrow Airport. I was picked up by my grandmother, who was known to be a "posh" lady; a woman of pride and prestige. She smiled and greeted me pleasantly, but appeared firm. My first instinct was that I had to be on my best behavior with her. She had a chauffeur, Vick, who escorted us from the airport to home. As we drove to wherever home was, I admired my new surroundings. First, I noticed that the airport was huge, bigger than any I had ever seen before. It was at that time that true socialization and integration took root in my life. It started there because it was the first time that I actually observed people from different cultures interacting, other than my own. I was now part of a bigger society. Curiously, I absorbed the sounds of the various languages being spoken along with the contrasting cultural styles and the colorful medley of ethnicities. I was in awe. As we commuted to my new home I observed the greenery around me; the beautiful mountain sides, and the fresh flowers that bloomed an array of colors. The streets looked squeaky clean. *The grass is greener on the other side* came alive at that very instance, but it was short lived as we soon approached other unsightly areas. I noticed homes that were unkept, with worn down structures, dirty roadways, and really old vehicles. I was surprised by the stark contrast, but in that moment I decided that my environment would not define me instead what I made of it would. My grandmother's beautiful townhouse was neatly tucked in a quiet and clean cul-de-sac. Inside was spotless, it was styled with modern furniture pieces, unique paintings decorated the walls and a glass nursery adorned the back of the house. The nursery was set up beautifully with a seating area on the inside and I immediately knew where I would be spending most of my time. My room was lovely, but the nursery gave me an outdoorsy feeling which reminded me very much of being back home. I was impressed.

Days later, she sat with me and expressed what she expected of me for the time I'd be residing with her. At first, I thought she was pretty strict, but as time progressed, I realized how much she helped to shape who I am today. It was because of her input that I developed into a more modest and self-disciplined individual. I have no regrets of my time spent in London and appreciate all the new experiences it opened up for me. I attended Royal Russell High in the Croydon area, and while attending school there I learned to interact with other cultures.

The first day of class I was dropped off by my chauffeur and directed to my classroom. My new classmates were of many different nationalities to include Africans, Indians, Chinese, Caucasians, Europeans along with other nationalities. The first day of class marked my moment of integration into a new country and region. After a year of being around diverse cultures, I began to truly embrace my own culture and heritage. I started to realize how important it was for me to represent my culture, be true to myself, and not shy away from my heritage, due to criticism, stereotypes, or prejudices. One day after school, while walking alone, I suddenly realized how privileged I was to be in another country where I could interact with other cultures and learn new ways and customs.

I believe exposure to other cultures and customs is an important part of a child's developmental. I was shy when I first started school because of my limited knowledge and exposure, but it only took me a few months to break that behavior as I built friendships and hung out with others. I began spending time with friends from Kenya, Nigeria, Zimbabwe, Europe and other Caribbean islands such as Antigua. I immediately took a liking to cultural diversity. I began reading many books concerning cultural religions, norms, habits and practices. I started to look outside my culture for friends. I also started to imagine having a mixed family of my own. I was open by the age of 16 to date males from different cultures.

Questions to Consider

- Have you traveled outside your birth area? If so, where have you been?

- What other cultures have you been exposed to, if any, and how has this exposure impacted you?

- Do you have friends or relatives from other cultural backgrounds?

- How important is cultural diversity to you and why or why not?

- Are you open to having a partner from another culture than your own? Why or why not?

Chapter Four

DATING EXPERIENCES: KNOW YOUR LIKES AND DISLIKES

Dating can be one of a girl's biggest challenges as she transitions throughout her life. There is always pressure to find the right person. For me, it was about finding someone who was loving, loyal, confident, ambitious, and most of all spiritual. My friends and family have always felt that I held unrealistic expectations and that the guy I was seeking didn't exist. They believed that I was too caught up with romance novels and TV shows, but I knew what I was seeking. I knew that I needed to break from what I was seeing around me; young single parents, broken relationships, and immature connections. I made one decision, which I believe to be the biggest decision of my life concerning relationships and that was not to have sex until I was married. Again, my friends and some younger family members thought I was being unrealistic. I remember making this decision on my grandmother's veranda when I was about 9 years old. I was sitting with a group of my cousins, and we were engaged in a discussion about our parents and our siblings; it dawned on us that no one had parents who were married, so I decided that I wasn't going down that road. Yes, I made that decision at 9 years old and I didn't regret it.

I had my very first boyfriend at the age of 19. I was tough concerning guys and their gestures towards me. Back in the seventh grade, I reported Michael to the principal's office because he touched my hand and told me that he liked me. Yes, silly but true. I was hardcore. I recall telling my first boyfriend that he had to meet certain requirements before I would call him my boyfriend. I remember asking him about his family, his goals, and what his intentions were concerning me. He had never been questioned like that before, but I was serious, because I had a plan. I felt that two individuals should have a concrete plan as they grow in a relationship, otherwise they are bound for failure.

My parents were pretty strict concerning my dating. They believed that I shouldn't concern myself with a boyfriend prior to the appropriate age for marriage— which in their eyes would be after I finished college. I remember telling my father about a boy when I was 18 years old and I recall feeling so nervous. I wasn't sure what he was going to say and as I expected he replied *"just keep focusing on your studies"*; so having a boyfriend was never a priority for me while in school. My family was also firm about me dating only guys who were spiritual. They believed someone spiritual would make a better companion, but how does one tell whether someone is really spiritual or not? I had many guys tell me they were spiritual that apparently were not. I knew based on their character and how they treated me that they were nowhere close to having good spiritual insight. I believe that spirituality is the connection that one has to their higher self and to the Divine and I believed that I deserved someone who possessed that special Connection. So, I took my sweet time in evaluating potential male interests. This trait was non-negotiable for me.

The longest relationship I was in before I got married lasted under one year and didn't last longer due to lack of commitment on his part. I felt that it was in my best interest to separate myself from someone who couldn't envision their future with me and a committed relationship after certain time had been invested. Indeed, the selection process was a tedious one, but coming from a woman who is now married… it was worth the wait. I strongly believe a woman should be clear and hold firm to what she values and expects.

I remember attending several Christian mix and mingle dating events and even hosting my very own Singles Ministry program and throughout the process not having a partner. I was about 25 years old when I was asked to be the Singles ministry leader within my religious organization at the time. I was told that I was chosen because I possessed certain qualities that a young woman in waiting should demonstrate. I was outgoing, respectful, loyal, courageous, helpful, kind, and assertive. I gave my first speech as a leader of the organization the same year that I was elected; I raised issues concerning girls not building the character of a wife prior to seeking a husband. I believe that as girls grow and mature they should shape their characters to attract the partners that they desire. **I began to realize that I had to become the person who I desired to be with**. I believe male and female function differently but their underlying character and or personalities can be very similar. I began working on myself.

For someone to attract the right person they must themselves first reflect the right character and spirit. I remember doing weekly challenges on becoming a better person; becoming more attentive, kind, a better listener, more forgiving, and a better communicator. It was an amazing learning experience throughout my single-hood. These exercises helped me to become a better partner. I spent about 5 years working on myself; shaping my character to attract the partner that I needed. As I worked on embodying the qualities which I believed were important, I also opened myself up to connect with others; building networks and other supportive relationships. I concentrated on building love and positive relationships overall and not just in one area.

However, within those five years of waiting to connect with the right partner, I also experienced some disappointing and discouraging moments. Nevertheless, I had to be strong enough to host the round table talks that served as a source of encouragement for other single women whom were seeking relationships. There were many wedding invitations from friend's who were marrying off—which didn't make things any better—but I still believed in myself and my future. I never gave up on finding a good partner. **I didn't compromise my standards, plans, or dreams.**

I remember scheduling a meeting with Malcolm, a man I dated, who seemed unclear about his feelings towards me. After about a year of his indecisiveness, I walked into his office and made one statement. I said, *"I don't know what you are doing, but I am a nice person and if you can't make up your mind concerning me this minute I am leaving and will never look back."* I gave him a few minutes to respond but he was still wavering and so I walked out. It took a lot of courage, because I really thought this guy would make the cut; he was hard working, intelligent, ambitious but didn't have a good eye for the right woman. I have no regrets. I believe that a girl should stand up for what she believes and have confidence in her decisions. My friends were quite surprised at what I did because they knew I really liked Malcolm. After that day, I focused and worked on my personal goals while still remaining open for new encounters.

I think the idea of living in New York City came with lots of expectations, but being in a bigger city didn't make dating any easier. It took the same effort as living in a rural area. So, I opened myself up to online dating at the age of 28 and that turned out to be quite a challenge. Online, guys typically claimed personalities and characteristics that they didn't possess. However, that was not always the case, as I met a young Nigerian doctor, online, who was my age. I thought I had scored a lucky draw until 3 months later I noticed the same patterns of behavior; inconsistent communications, lack of focus, immature behaviors, and a low priority for relationship building. He wasn't ready for a meaningful relationship. It was shortly after that break up that I met my husband-to-be.

Questions to Consider

- What standards/criteria do you have in place for your ideal mate to meet?

- Identify 5 traits that you would like to see in your ideal mate?

- What is your dating style? How do you define dating?

- Are there any rules or terms that you have set as a boundary during your dating experiences?

- Have you ever had to walk away from a relationship that wasn't working, and if so, how did you identify the areas that weren't right for you?

Chapter Five

FAMILY RELATIONS & MARRIAGE BELIEFS: DO YOU SHARE THE SAME BELIEFS?

I grew up in a single parent household. My mother and father met when they were much younger and my mother had me at 19 years old. She has always told me how being alone shaped her independent nature. She shared with me that she had two marriage proposals of which she refused both. She explained that the timing seemed off and how she believed that one of them should have been with another woman. She further explained that she didn't feel she deserved his love while he had another who was vying for his love. I believe there was a deep sense of pride mixed with a lack of confidence that my mother battled with which caused her to abandon any pursuit for lasting love. The second proposal came from a man that she met in a religious setting after moving to New York City. Once again, she rejected the proposal and justified her actions by reporting that she didn't think he was serious after nearly two years of friendship. I couldn't understand why she passed up on these opportunities to love and grow with someone as opposed to being alone. She sounded indifferent and somehow pleased about making her own decisions. She liked not having to answer to anyone else. As I connected with my maternal and paternal family members and observed their relationships, I realized that only one or two of them were married. I had aunts and uncles who preferred cohabiting. I remember when I was younger, I had asked Auntie Denise why she hadn't married after living with her boyfriend for more than eight years and she replied, "*marriage is hard and one must commit themselves to it.*" She later went on to say, "*once married, the couple can fall out of love*" and she didn't want that pressure. I was about twelve years old at the time, I just couldn't understand. I believe if a couple lives together without being married it's the same level of commitment that could also lead to "falling out of love." Even after listening to her story, I still determined to get married and not create a family out of wedlock. I know that marriage is not considered as necessary or as sacred to some people, but I still believe in its sanctity. I believe a family should be started on the foundation of marriage. Marriage has an impact on family and the quality of their lives if the two truly love and admire each other. As I watched my mother raise my brother and I, the feeling that life could have been better if our fathers were in our home made sense because what one parent could not provide the other parent would be able to. I have always admired married couples and their children. They always appeared to have a sense of belonging with and to each other as one unit.

The number of marriages in my extended family can be counted on one hand, up to this very day. I am not judging this as bad or good because I feel that everyone has the right to their own lives and choices. I was raised to focus on my studies so that I could excel and gain my own independence which was very good, but I still felt that something was missing. I was never trained or taught on building relationships. I was never advised on the type of relationship to build for the purpose of connecting with the right partner, that would encourage growth or further achievement. I remember moving to New York City to reconnect with my mother and, even though I was an adult at the time, her first piece of advise to me was, *"be careful who you talk to."* Caution is always needed to be safe, but if one remains cautious without a balance of openness to connect with others then they will limit their destiny and even a chance to find a partner. She advised me to maintain my independence (an independence that didn't work for her), based on the results of her life and experiences. I was determined to break the cycle of broken families and broken relationships. Parents from my small island believe that what they say is set in stone and if not taken seriously will bring a sense of suffering or pain. I on the other hand, believe that our concepts and ideas can change daily as we grow and expand. I was about 24 years old when I moved to reconnect with her after not having seen her since my teenage years. My travels have certainly helped me to expand my knowledge and views concerning life. When I moved from the island I became culture sensitive. I was no longer defined by any one concept or belief. I became open to building and sharing. I dedicated most of my twenties catering to the needs of others, especially to my dear mother, and it didn't go well once I made the significant decision to enter the role of marriage. Some parents from my very beautiful native island tend to have a false sense of obligation in the lives of their children, even when their children are adults. I observed this with my friends and with younger cousins and their parents but didn't fully understand it until it happened to us. I spent most of my twenties serving and helping various members of my family. I was young and single, so this wasn't a problem for me at the time. I would date at intervals, but nothing serious, so it didn't have a major effect on the amount of time I spent with family, especially with my sickly mother. I cherished all the moments I spent with family and I adored the connection. I felt that as I built relationships and supported my family that naturally those moments would be appreciated and cherished once I was no longer able to commit the same amount of time, but that was not the case. There was an expectation to spend the same amount of time with close relatives, and if it wasn't met, it would be referenced as a lack of love for family. I believe that the good you do should naturally return to you through those you gave kindness to or through other means. I was hurt and surprised after years of supporting my relatives that I didn't get the same support in return during the time that I focused on building my own family. In building a new relationship that is geared towards marriage one must make time to nurture and develop that bond in order for it to be meaningful and long lasting.

Questions to Consider

- What are your family's views on marriage and relationships?

- In observing your extended family, does your family have more married or unmarried adults?

- How much involvement do your friends and family have on your relationships? Is this a healthy amount?

- What, if any, differing views from your family do you hold concerning marriage and relationships?

Chapter Six

OUR UNION: CHOOSING YOUR MATE WITHOUT EXTERNAL INFLUENCES

My husband, Jason, and I met on a bright summer day. We met at the workplace. I was assigned to a patient who happened to have Jason as his nurse. I was surprised to have met Jason because I had visited the facility several times before and had never been introduced to him. It wasn't until after my third visit there that Jason began inquiring about my life. He didn't hesitate to ask me if I was in a relationship. On our first phone conversation, we spoke for several hours; there was something about him I found intriguing. We spoke at length that day, but once Jason found out that I was already committed to another person he respected my commitment. It was shortly after I broke up with my boyfriend that Jason contacted me again to say hello. That was about six weeks later on the fourth of July weekend and he was ecstatic to learn that I was no longer involved. We went out that same weekend to a nice romantic dinner and all went well. I was excited to see early on that he possessed several characteristics that I admired in a partner. After several long conversations and interactions Jason was ready to date exclusively; I, on the other hand wanted to wait. I had him wait for about 2 weeks before I was ready to make that level of commitment. He is a very respectable man. He helped me tap into parts of myself that I would usually shy away from or wasn't even aware of. He is open to cultural diversity which attracted me to him even more. I had said I wouldn't date a man from my small island because I had my own stereotypes. I was wrong. It doesn't matter where an individual is from, what matters is who he becomes. He is a partner that adds great value to my world, one who I can grow with and experience a fuller aspect of life with. This journey of being married is something that I have longed for since I was a young girl. I wanted to start a family as a married unit. I am traditional when it comes to this aspect of life, but pretty liberal in other areas. I had waited seven years to be in a committed relationship. Within this time frame, I spent time getting to know myself and exactly what I wanted in a male partner. I started to interact with older married women who had been married for several years to inquire about their union and their success. I spent time reading materials regarding marriage and relationships. I read materials on the topics of being a good wife and or partner; spending time going to seminars on marriage and relationships. I spent much time in preparation.

    I was honored to have a man who I admired asked me to be his wife. We dated for about four months before he asked me to be his wife. I felt that it was too soon, but he thought differently. He knew exactly what he wanted, and he wanted to secure it before it was too late. My family thought that this engagement was too early as well, but then later thought that the date we set to be married was too far away. I took time away to meditate and listen to my own inner voice because I understood that only I could make this decision for my future, no one else. Even though my family felt they had the best of intentions at heart, I made the decision to move forward despite their oppositions. According to my family, there is a certain time and order in which things should be done, but I believe that every individual and situation is different, no one method fits every situation. I was happy to know that I was ready, and I had a partner who I felt strongly about. We had some differences, but most of all we shared commonalities that made us stronger every day.

Our courtship was an amazing experience; we had weekly events and activities planned just to get to know each other. We hung out almost every day and after a short time we felt that we knew each other longer than we actually did. We spent a great deal of time sharing the deeper details of our lives respectively. We also spent time after several months, going to marriage seminars and watching videos on building good marriage relationships prior to our engagement. I learned that Jason enjoyed cooking, he spent a great deal of time, weekly, preparing me authentic dishes from various cultures such as Jamaican, American, Italian and Asian cuisine. We both enjoyed the outdoors and doing service within our community. We are both in the nursing field and that has also connected us on many levels as we are both passionate about helping others. I find my husband to be very talented and ambitious, and we both strive for success in many areas of our lives. Notice how this all goes back to chapter one. It is vital to the success of a relationship to share common values and beliefs. Don't just hear what they say, but is the evidence of what they speak visible in their lives and interactions?

We were engaged after four months and married after about a year and a half. We had a destination wedding so we chose our beautiful island of birth, Jamaica. Again, many family members objected to a destination wedding because they preferred a local area for family members to attend, but many just weren't willing to assist in making it possible. Therefore, we continued as planned with our destination wedding and had an amazing experience with the friends and family who did support us. We enjoy visiting and learning about different cultures and so we honeymooned in Medellin, Colombia. We took a road trip across our small island, something that we both wanted to do prior to our connection, and we did it together. It was unique and different. We have visited other areas such as Mexico, Bahamas, Columbia, South America and various areas of the United States. We both enjoy traveling and we have similar interests to continue our travels to various parts of the world such as South Africa, Asia, and Europe. It is very important for you and your partner to share common interests. I was very skeptical concerning the kind of guy I would attract due to my teachings and the things I heard within our family circle, but I later realized in life that it was all up to me. I had to choose someone who would suit "my" personality and vice versa.

My husband and I spent a great deal of time together before we knew that we were right for each other. We knew the bottom line; that we loved each other and that we believed in a higher power to guide our relationship. Just like anything in life nothing is ever certain, but I believed that I was being led by a greater source and I followed my heart. Many family members had opinions as to what they felt was right or wrong , however experiences can be used as a guide to prevent mishaps and create a plan for better outcomes. I respect the different family dynamics and in observation I have chosen the best structure for my life and future. My husband and I are working on developing our own structure that will focus on building a strong family connection, and maintaining a positive spirit and energy. We strive every day to be the most that we could be…both individually and as a couple.

I would like to share the wedding vows we made to each other which left a significant impact on us both.

My Vows:
Within this path of life, our hearts yearn to be with our twin flame, our chosen one, our supporter, our best friend; to be with the one who can love me as I love. It was with tears in my eyes on bended knees that I asked my Divine Lord about my other half. It was no sooner that I asked, that I found my missing link (my husband). A link that would connect me even closer to the Divine, a link that helped me to be my greater self, a link that makes me smile and even makes me cry, and makes me laugh; eliciting all my emotions in ways no other could even dare to try. A link that treats me like royalty; a Queen.

I found my lover, my supporter, my best friend, my prayer partner and my travel buddy. I promise to love him from the deepest parts of my heart. We have God as our guide through every avenue of our lives in good times and yes in bad times too. We have grown so much together. We have challenged each other to be better, and we have been since the day we met. God has smiled on us and for this, all is well. I love you now and forever...

His Vows:
If someone told me two years ago I would have been in this position marrying my beautiful bride, I would have never believed it. However, from the moment we met I believe a new part of me was awakened, I started to believe whole-heartedly in this concept, this idea we call love. Because of my belief in this concept, this idea, this love, I started to imagine a life with you (my wife) by my side. I remembered, especially in the first few dates daydreaming meanwhile being in the same room with you. Now it is tangible you and I are here today getting married, now I trust that we continue to break more barriers, conquer even more adversaries all with the power of this love. Let us continue to be loyal to our dreams. I want us to always remember what it took to get to this moment, I want

us to always remember to follow our heart and not the mistaken concepts of others. I want you to continue to be who you truly are because that is who I love. Always stay committed to better, to our beliefs all while pushing the boundaries to what we can do with our marriage. My love, you know I do not gamble but I feel you gave me a hunch to bet it all on you. I will never look back now, with you, I choose to go forward. I trust that our love will last, I trust that you were made just for me. I do and will love you.

Questions to Consider

- Where did you meet your partner?
- What value has your partner added to your life?

- What value have you added to theirs?

- Do you and your partner share any similarities concerning family views on relationships and marriage? What are the similarities and what are the differences?

If you are not in a relationship currently:

- Whats are some ideal settings in which you envision meeting your partner?

- What value would you like a partner to add to your life?

- What value would you add to theirs?

- What views on building healthy relationships/marriage are you looking for them to possess?

Chapter Seven

SECURING OUR UNION: STAYING COMMITTED AND TRUE TO EACH OTHER

I believe in life that there is no greater thing than to be guided by a higher spiritual power. Many would ask what or who that higher power is, in my case it's the most High God. Many people interpret God in different ways. Many refer to him by different names. I once believed that he was masculine, but now I believe God is all in all, with no one identity. I remember referring to or praying to a higher power since the tender age of 7. I was taught about God and his power from a young age by my grandparents and my parents. I involved God in everything I did, from the simplest to the most complex of things. I was always advised to remain prayerful on issues involving myself and others. I earnestly believe in the power of prayer to transform any situation. I also believe that there is nothing impossible for the Highest Power to resolve. I believe that if anyone starts a foundation with the Most

High as the root and source of what they do that they cannot go wrong. I ask for direction in everything that I do and so therefore the direction to choose and marry the right partner was not an exception. I remember praying as a teenager about not following the wrong company which would lead me to connect with the wrong individuals. I strongly believe that the environments one chooses to dwell amongst will have an impact on the outcome on their lives. I made a vow to myself when I was 9 years old never to have intercourse until I was married. I grew tired of seeing broken families and young girls taking on responsibilities of parenthood before they were mentally and financially equipped to do so. I strongly advise young adults to live their lives to the fullest at every stage of their youth before taking on bigger responsibilities. I was told that I was being unrealistic, but I stayed committed to my dreams. One must have a goal every step of their journey to stay focused and true to self. It's important to set goals, so that one is not easily misdirected to an undesirable path. I asked the higher power to direct me in every potential relationship so that I could make the right selection. I didn't care if I was talking to the person for the first time or the last time, it was my duty to seek direction and not waste any aspect of my life. **I spent a great deal of time praying within the first few weeks of meeting someone; I called it the "is he worth my time segment".** Believe it or not, I normally get a response or an inclination within the first 30 days or less. I met my husband when I was 30 years old and I knew within 2 weeks that he was worth my time and within 4 months that he was an interesting, unique, God-fearing and loving person. I am still spending time getting to understand him even now being married, so I am not saying that you will know the person right away. I am saying that it is very important to seek divine guidance to assist in making the right choices for your future. I knew that my husband was the one after evaluating the way he treated me and connecting it with my own concept of how I should be treated. I knew he was the one after looking back and recalling the type of guy I desired; he exhibited many of the traits I sought. I knew he was the one because we had a lot of similarities and most of all we shared common ground with our faith and belief. We both believe that God is all powerful and that for us to inspire others we must reflect a Christ-like attitude. We both believe in the power of conversion and the need to display positive attributes in everything that we do.

I spent about seven years asking for direction and guidance concerning my partner and God's desire for me and my future. I asked God for a special person who would display certain attributes and who would be God fearing. I was repeatedly asked by several friends and family when I was going to meet someone and get married, and although I couldn't answer them at the time, I kept my faith. I knew one day that it was going to happen. I just didn't know when. I felt sad at times after I had reached a certain age and wasn't married. I kept in constant prayer. I had many single ladies say to me that if I wasn't actively looking for a mate it would just happen, but I learned that wasn't true. I spent a great deal of my time believing that theory and it didn't work. It wasn't until I made it crystal clear that I was a young, vibrant, and intelligent female looking for an eligible bachelor that it hit home with me that I needed to be conscious about what I desired for in order for it to manifest into my world. I didn't display any anxiety about it, I simply made it known. I began to convey more confidence and less self-consciousness, in my appearance, behavior and communication style.

It wasn't until about 4 years prior to meeting my husband that I changed my concepts regarding dating. I once held a strong belief that the partner whom I chose had to work in a higher profession than myself. I was very independent and I wasn't going to be committed to a man who didn't have their own home and be ready to marry within a few years. I began realizing that all these concepts didn't work and that I needed to be open. **It wasn't until I changed my misconceptions about what I needed in a partner that I found my partner.**

My husband and I spent a great deal of time reflecting and meditating to gain divine direction concerning our lives and our future. We believe that God brought us together for a reason and we spend every moment fulfilling that plan. We secure our union by staying conscious of the divine order in our lives, being true to self and doing the best we can in every way. We are seen as a unique couple. We respect everyone's beliefs and concepts, but we spend time reading and developing our own concepts and beliefs. We know that life is constantly evolving and therefore nothing is set in stone. We believe that God can use anything and anyone to make a difference.

As a couple, we resolve issues amongst each other within our home; it is very important not to involve others to decide on your relationship issues. It is imperative to take time out and think about how you should handle the situation because only you and your spouse can decide on your relationship.

Questions to Consider

- How has your spiritual belief system impacted your relationship?

- Do you and your partner share the same spiritual beliefs, and if not, what the are the main differences?

- How do these differences, if any, help to shape your expectations of them?

- Do your spiritual practices/beliefs have any impact on choosing a partner, and if so, how?

If you are currently not in a relationship:

- Do you believe that your spiritual practices will have an impact on your relationship?

- Do you believe that partners should share similar beliefs, and if so, why?

- How has your spirituality shaped you for your ideal partner?

Chapter Eight

SUMMARY: MAINTAINING A HEALTHY RELATIONSHIP

It is truly an amazing experience when two individuals inspire and strengthen each other. It is known that some women are the strong, confident, and independent types. I was considered to be one of those types, but what drives my womanhood is to be identified as a queen, a wife, a good mother, a good friend, a good family member, and a successful professional woman. I think that being asked to be a wife to someone I truly admire, is one of the most amazing encounters I have ever had. It was inspired by the love and the beauty we saw in each other and he asked me to marry within four months of us dating, because he couldn't wait for us to connect on a deeper level. I had waited so long for the moment and it had finally arrived. I had been told that I had too many restrictions and standards. I was told maybe it wasn't God's plan for me to marry, but I'm writing now to say those were all lies; you can never set your standard too high for the love you believe you deserve. God's will for you is to give you a "good and expected end," and never to harm you. Believing in the myths created by family or culture will never get you exactly what you need for your life. It is best to have a biblical foundation from which to develop your beliefs concerning relationships. I am mindful of constructive family beliefs and culture, yet at the same time I have also learned how to develop and honor my own concepts. If you desire success in your relationships, you must first understand why you are in a relationship and then identify what you expect from it.

To secure your union:

- The couple must understand each other's background. Learning the dynamics of each other's childhood is fundamental in understanding their personality and behavioral patterns.
- The couple must discuss their own experiences when it comes to socialization, their exposure to different cultures and beliefs system.
- It's important to discuss previous dating experiences and develop a plan as to how the couple will prevent repetition of unhealthy habits or patterns that they disliked in previous relationships.
- Family plays an integral role in the relationship, so the couple must identify family patterns and cultural norms that they will accept or reject within their relationship.
- The couple must develop a faith-based system that assists them in building a strong foundation where they receive good direction and guidance.
- The couple must keep conflict and resolution issues amongst themselves, instead of inviting third parties into the relationship to provide solutions.
- The couple should be assisting each other to grow and expand in every way possible.

Questions to Consider

- What have you learned concerning marriage and relationships from your own experiences that may differ from your familial or cultural beliefs or norms?

- What key qualities would you say are needed to build strong relationships?

- List 5 ways in which you will contribute to securing your relationship and/or marriage?

  1. _____
  2. _____
  3. _____
  4. _____
  5. _____

Having worked through these chapters and taking the time to answer each of these questions, should give you some confidence in moving forward and building a lasting relationship.

FINAL THOUGHTS

I wrote this book to share our story and it's our desire to inspire young married women and men to secure their union and make their own decisions concerning relationships. I also want to advise single men and women to seek a Higher powers' guidance to connect and marry the right person. If it is your desire to attain a lasting and healthy marriage, you will. I strongly believe that when you find someone that can love you and connect with you to share a life, it's a gift, and so treasure it. I have always desired to break the cycle of broken families and single parenthood. Although I am the product of one, the change began with me. I believe in the sacredness of marriage and the powerful bond of family.

Notes

Notes

Notes

Notes

ABOUT THE AUTHOR

TAMEIKA ALLEN DAVIS was born and raised in the beautiful Caribbean and is a Family Nurse Practitioner, within the state of Florida, where she presently resides. Having come through her own set of experiences, and breaking free from the cultural norms of her Caribbean background, in addition to serving as a singles ministry counselor and singles event director for many years has prepared Mrs. Davis in finding her passion in helping others find healthy and lasting relationships.

"It was not until I realized all relationships took on their own form and I had the power to attain what I desired, that I released the skepticism and opened myself up to new possibilities. As I conducted seminars, I was being transformed by the different topics and discussion and so I am now able to share with you my experience and why you too can make that change."